T0160609

Haikus
for
New
York
City

Dedicated to the people of
New York City

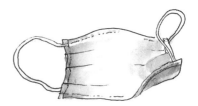

Haikus

for

New York City

By Peter C. Goldmark, Jr.
Illustrations by Sandra Goldmark

TUTTLE Publishing

Tokyo | Rutland, Vermont | Singapore

Preface

I started writing poetry fairly regularly when I was 40 years old. I wrote for myself, not for others. It was a way to find meaning in what was going on in the world around me; it brought some depth and aesthetic context to a life that was always intense, often chaotic, and occasionally superficial.

I have held positions of great responsibility and sometimes had to handle difficult crises—riots, strikes, once a hostage situation. Pressure and crises can harden and numb you if you do not have a way to find meaning in your life, if you do not remain free to think and to experience all sorts of feelings. Writing poetry does that for me.

The haiku is a poem that has exactly 17 syllables. Many verses have a "pivot," or a turning point, where the haiku changes direction or surprises the reader. I have heard many arguments about what form the haiku ought to take in English: three lines of 5, 7 and 5 syllables respectively as the classical English form of the haiku has it? Some other pattern?

In Japanese, all haikus are a single horizontal or vertical series of Japanese characters (*hiragana* and *kanji*). So I figured all the huffing and puffing about the proper English form was irrelevant. We should deploy the 17 syllables in English as each of us sees fit.

About four years ago, I found myself writing several haiku about New York City. I liked the puzzle-like assembly of short, measured pictures of and insights into the large, multi-dimensional city I call home. And then as 2019 and 2020 unfolded, both our country and our city came under stress. The adventure in self-government in America began to wobble seriously. Then the COVID pandemic hit. All this made me realize how much I loved and valued my city—its beauty, its diversity, its remarkable people, its grit and resilience... and how fragile and unique it was.

One day a friend said: "You've got to publish these, Peter." I talked with my daughter, Sandra, a writer and wonderful visual artist. She encouraged me. I asked her if she would do the drawings. She is amazingly busy—but she said yes.

I decided to do it. And that is why you are holding this book in your hands—because it is a timely celebration of a unique and wonderful city and its people, written to honor the ties and realities that bind them together.

I love the City and I owe it a lot. The City needs all of us now

Peter C. Goldmark, J
December 202

Four cabled bridges stand
over the churning
East River
like lifelines.

For the sea, one shared tidal network.

For us, three rivers and a sound.

Put away your

      crampons,

            pith helmets,

               compass,

                    bug spray

—won't need 'em here.

Remember:

    people came

        to this brawling city

           for a better life.

A magic gift,

     that statue of the lady in the harbor,

        arm raised,

            quietly telling us something

              central and vital about ourselves

Almost two million people live here,
four million work here

—Manhattan.

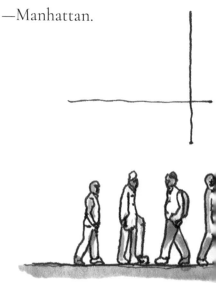

How can so much

    wealth,

        ambition

            and talent

   fit on one small island?

Ever go one entire day

crossing only

at the corners on green?

Cables,

    sewers,

        mains,

            steampipes,

                gas lines

—underground tangle we don't see.

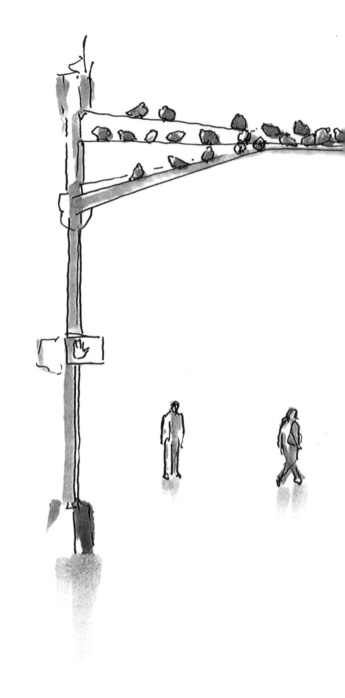

In this city

    of crowds,

        horns,

            shoving,

                hurrying,

you can be alone.

In New York a glance will tell

    if you can talk with someone

        you don't know.

Others think New Yorkers

are wise-asses.

We're just being descriptive.

New York City can

    stretch,

        energize,

            push,

                excite,

                    teach,

                        preach,

                            and reveal.

New York City does not often
gently calm you down,
reach out and heal.

New York offers you contrasts:

heat and cold,

haste and pleasure,

pain and joy.

A square but rolling, friendly valley

between concrete cliffs

—Central Park.

Anyone can go in the parks.

Everyone comes out.

You can sleep,

read,

dream,

bike,

skate,

pray,

fly kites,

write verse,

smell flowers,

sing,

run

or vegetate.

Weekends.

The noise of the park-goers

nearly drowns out

police sirens.

Wall Street

    cloaked in shadows.

        Bayonne Bridge

           arched against the red horizon.

High the Palisades,

     parted from their other half in West Africa

by a river,

     an island,

       an ocean

        and a million centuries.

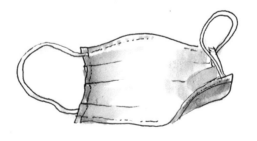

Covidiously empty

    streets,

        shutters,

            locks

—our old city is ill.

Police,

    fire,

        sanitation,

            bus and subway workers,

                hospital staff

—they became an essential

    nervous system

        after New York was born.

But the city could no longer exist

if our front line

was not here.

Neighborhoods change,

rents rise,

stores that were always there

are gone overnight.

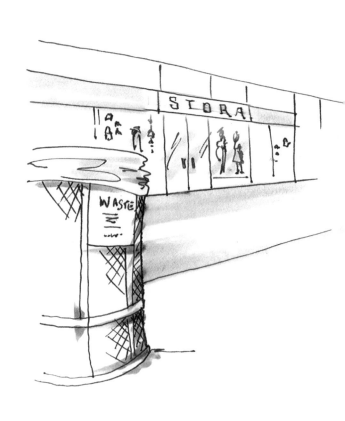

Rivers,

    traffic,

       fashion,

         news,

            investment

—things never stop flowing here.

"There is a train directly

behind this one."

New York City bullshit.

Hope?

Despair?

Forced courtesy?

Glances from the homeless

on the sidewalk.

No matter how fast you walk

in New York

someone always

strides past you.

DANGER
HIGH
VOLTAGE

If you press hard enough

things will shift,

breaks will come

—opportunity.

The quietest moments in New York
are the hours just before dawn.

Traffic lights blinking in reflective cycles
on still, deserted streets.

Stern buildings gazing down
on bare avenues
through lifeless window panes.

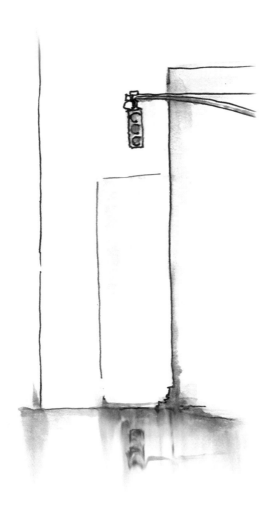

Tragically we're missing

a stethoscopic imagination.

Otherwise we could hear

the deafening drumroll

of nine million hearts.

All the city lights

cannot shut out

the full moon

over Prospect Park.

You can't rush it or chase it.

But sometimes in New York

peace will find you.

"Books to Span the East and West"

Tuttle Publishing was founded in 1832 in the small New England town of Rutland, Vermont [USA]. Our core values remain as strong today as they were then—to publish best-in-class books which bring people together one page at a time. In 1948, we established a publishing office in Japan—and Tuttle is now a leader in publishing English-language books about the arts, languages and cultures of Asia. The world has become a much smaller place today and Asia's economic and cultural influence has grown. Yet the need for meaningful dialogue and information about this diverse region has never been greater. Over the past seven decades, Tuttle has published thousands of books on subjects ranging from martial arts and paper crafts to language learning and literature—and our talented authors, illustrators, designers and photographers have won many prestigious awards. We welcome you to explore the wealth of information available on Asia at **www.tuttlepublishing.com**.

Published by Tuttle Publishing, an imprint of Periplus Editions (HK) Ltd.

www.tuttlepublishing.com

Text and Design Copyright © 2021 by Peter C. Goldmark, Jr.
Illustrations Copyright © 2021 by Sandra Goldmark

Book and website design by Hallie Easley and Evan Sargent of COMMIT. www.commitbranding.com

www.haikusfornyc.com

Distributed by:

North America, Latin America & Europe
Tuttle Publishing
364 Innovation Drive
North Clarendon, VT 05759-9436
Tel: (802) 773 8930; Fax: (802) 773 6993
info@tuttlepublishing.com
www.tuttlepublishing.com

Asia Pacific
Berkeley Books Pte Ltd
3 Kallang Sector #04-01
Singapore 349278
Tel: (65) 6741 2178; Fax: (65) 6741 2179
inquiries@periplus.com.sg

First Edition   ISBN 978-0-8048-5457-3

24 23 22 21   7 6 5 4 3 2

Printed in Malaysia on recycled paper   2105VP

RECYCLED
Paper made from recycled material
FSC™ C084469

TUTTLE PUBLISHING® is a registered trademark of Periplus Editions (HK) Ltd.